Angels
Predictions
2024

Rubi Astrólogas

Published Independently

All rights reserved © 2024.

Astrologers: Alina A. Rubi and Angeline Rubi

Email: rubiediciones29@gmail.com

Editing: Angeline A. Rubi

rubiediciones29@gmail.com

Introduction

This 2024 Angel Horoscope has many spiritual messages for you. If you feel lost, or if you are wondering what your mission is this year 2024, here you can find the answers. If you bought this book, it is because the universe is trying to tell you what to do and where to go. All you need is to discover the hidden messages that the Angels have sent you inside this book.

Sometimes we are so deep in a life with so much stress, that we forget that we are accompanied by beings of light, who are waiting for us to ask for help. When we are aware of their presence and decide to enjoy the gift of having them in our lives, our world is filled with magic.

Angels are beings of light; their mission is to help us to evolve and to protect us from dangers. All people are protected by an Angel, or several Angels, according to their date of birth. Your guardian Angel assures you success in love, work, and other areas of your life.

Angels have existed for thousands of years, in diverse cultures and civilizations. They have special powers and have contributed to human evolution, changes, and development of our society. The Guardian Angels will be present in your life during 2024 to protect you, strengthen your connections with the spiritual world, and to give you many miracles.

Archangel for your Zodiac Sign

Each zodiac sign has an Archangel mentor who oversees it.

When the time comes to reincarnate, we select the most appropriate zodiac sign to learn the life lessons that will bring us more experiences for our evolution.

The Archangels help us to choose the sign of the zodiac to fulfill the purposes of our soul.

Aries. Archangel Chamuel

The Archangel Chamuel means "the one who sees God", he is related to initiatives and passion, two super strong qualities in people of the Aries sign. This sign is tireless and does not stop until it achieves its goals.

The Archangel Chamuel gives Aries the power of decision and enthusiasm to accomplish his goals. This Archangel is also known as Samael, Chamuel or Camuel, and is the Angel of harmony, confidence, power, and diversity.

This Archangel gives the Aries sign an assertive and reliable personality.

Aries is an extroverted sign, impetuous and enthusiastic when it comes to taking on challenges. They are impatient and easily annoyed, but they are not resentful.

To Archangel Chamuel belongs the Golden Ray, the planet Mars, and the day Tuesday.

Archangel Chamuel's message for Aries is:

Only the energy of love within a purpose gives lasting value and benefit.

Rose quartz is related to the healing energies of Archangel Chamuel, and you can use them to heal yourself emotionally by invoking his name, or his presence, because he specializes in emotional healing.

Archangel Chamuel oversees all the Angels of Love. They give Aries when he asks for it, compassion, and love. Chamuel can help you with your relationships, specifically if you have conflicts, emotional complications, or breakups. Archangel Chamuel can help you find your soul or twin flame and in all circumstances that demand spontaneous communication.

Chamuel can help you build solid and healthy structures, improve your abilities to love, so that you have the capacity to give and receive love completely without conditions.

Chamuel dissolves feelings of low self-esteem, helps you find your purpose and soul mission.

The Archangel Chamuel represents the strength to face and overcome challenges in our lives. If you do not know what you want, Chamuel will move you to environments that will bring you peace, helping you to release tensions and stress. Archangel Chamuel is the protector of the weak and the humiliated.

As the Archangel Chamuel sees in all directions of time, i.e., three-dimensionally, he can help you find things you have lost.

Invoke the Archangel Chamuel if you feel sad, he will help you heal, relieve your pain and your inability to forgive.

To invoke or evoke help to heal emotionally with Archangel Chamuel you must light pink candles or put pink roses to ask for healing.

All Archangels have an exclusive place in the etheric plane of the Earth, and you can find their sanctuaries through meditation or in your dreams. The etheric temple of Archangel Chamuel is in St. Louis, Missouri, United States.

Taurus. Archangel Haniel

The Archangel Haniel rules the sign of Taurus, he refers to the characteristics of wholeness, confidence, and pragmatism. The Archangel Haniel's name means 'grace of God' and he is the Angel of intellectuality.

Haniel is related to the planet Venus, and the day Friday.

Taurus is a sign that loves material comfort, enjoys luxury, and quality goods. They are prosperous in many areas, but especially in finances.

Taurus is a very controlling sign that must learn patience. They possess a natural inclination towards stability but must be careful not to fall into the trap of materialism.

The Archangel Haniel is also known as Anael, Anafiel, and Daniel. His colors are orange and white.

This Archangel is related to the white and orange Ray.

Haniel has an energy that motivates us to seek spiritual wisdom, being also the Angel of Celestial Communication works with group energies and speakers. He is an

Archangel related to the Moon that is why he connects with us through visualizations and recurring dreams. Archangel Haniel helps transmute dark vibrations and energies and offers protection. He is with us in new beginnings when transitional stages happen in our lives.

This Archangel brings inspiration to our lives, teaches lessons and oversees spiritual healing, and diverse types of religions. Archangel Haniel retrieves lost secrets, harmonizes relationships, and brings beauty in everything. Haniel heals envy, anger, and jealousy.

Archangel Haniel provides you with information about your profession, and relationships. He assists you in your spiritual journey and urges you to seek your life's purpose. He urges you to look within yourself and find your personal truth because in this way you can stand up for yourself.

Archangel Haniel helps you to live in the present, see reality and recognize your talents and abilities.

Archangel Haniel reminds you that it is your responsibility to be healthy mentally and physically. This Archangel is related to healing through quartz and essential oils, which is why he oversees homeopathic physicians. This powerful

Archangel possesses the power to transform sadness into happiness.

This Archangel works with imbalances in the energy field and brings healing on an emotional, spiritual, and physical level.

This is a warrior Archangel who helps us fulfill our soul's purpose, guiding us through revelations, visions, and angelic synchronicities.

When you feel confused or depressed, invoke the Archangel Haniel to give you the gift of perseverance.

Gemini. Archangel Raphael

Gemini is protected by the Archangel Raphael, which is why this zodiac sign is so adaptable and sociable.

Raphael is one of the main healing angels and guides the healers.

Archangel Raphael rules the planet Mercury and the day Wednesday.

People of the Gemini sign are highly intelligent, their most valuable tool is their mind. Gemini is very versatile, and this attitude drains his energies leading him sometimes to nervous exhaustion and anxiety. Gemini people have an insatiable thirst for learning and their minds are very curious.

Archangel Raphael is related to the Green Ray. Raphael's healing powers are focused on dissolving blockages by transmuting them into love.

Archangel Raphael is known to be the chief of the Guardian Angels and is the patron of medicine, hence he is also called the Archangel of Knowledge.

Raphael is also the patron saint of travelers and assists in the spiritual and physical healing not only of humans, but also of animals.

This Archangel Raphael can help you develop your intuition and enhance your creative visualization. It puts you in touch with your personal spirituality and allows you to find healing in nature. Emerald is the healing quartz related to Archangel Raphael.

Archangel Raphael works in your subconscious so that you can free yourself from fear and darkness. The Healing Angels team is led by Archangel Raphael, these energies of Archangel Raphael and his Healing Angels can be invoked in hospitals and in circumstances where there is a sick person who is not known to have an illness.

Archangel Raphael focuses his healing energies on dissolving blockages in the chakras that cause disease and helps to eliminate addictions.

Rafael heals the wounds of past lives, erasing all inherited family karmas.

You can call Archangel Raphael every time you, another person has a physical illness, he will intervene directly and guide you to effect healing.

Archangel Raphael reminds you that it is through forgiveness that healing occurs, and he is intricately connected to the healers of light. Raphael ensures that all that is necessary appears to facilitate successful healing.

Call upon Archangel Raphael to protect and guide you, he will help you to cleanse your energies and focus. To invoke the healing power of Archangel Raphael, light green or yellow candles and you will receive instant results.

Archangel Raphael is not restricted by the limitations of time and space, being able to be simultaneously with all who invoke his presence. He comes to your side the instant you ask for help.

Cancer - Archangel Gabriel

The Archangel Gabriel protects the sign of Cancer. He rules on Monday.

Cancer is supervised is a very empathetic and sensitive sign. They look gentle, but they are active. Family is the most important thing for Cancer.

The Archangel Gabriel is known as the Angel of the Resurrection, the Angel of harmony and joy. He announced the birth of Jesus Christ and communicated with Joan of Arc.

Archangel Gabriel teaches you to seek angelic help through meditation and dreams and takes care of humanity.

Gabriel is the Archangel of the mind, you can call on him when you have mental challenges, to help you make decisions.

Archangel Gabriel is the protector of emotions, and creativity. When we struggle with abuse, addictions, dysfunctional families, and to have love it is Archangel Gabriel that we must invoke.

Archangel Gabriel offers you spirituality and uplifts your spirit. He alerts you to be aware of the energies around you.

Gabriel knows your soul purpose and mission; his mission is to help you understand what your contract obligations are in this incarnation.

Archangel Gabriel increases creativity, optimism, transmutes fears and gives you motivation. Gabriel cleanses and raises your vibrations, guides you in your life and helps you to live faithfully, honoring your talents and abilities.

Gabriel reminds you that everyone contributes to the development of humanity by being who they are. He wants you to be firm in your convictions.

This Archangel will help you to know the truth in conflict situations, he will give you more intuition and insight.

Archangel Gabriel is an Angel of knowledge, has connection with spiritual leaders, and instructs us on what our talents are and shows you the symbols of your soul's mission so that you will be able to attract perfect connections and opportunities.

Call upon Archangel Gabriel to cleanse and purify your body and mind of negative thoughts. Call upon him for help with all forms of communication, including the ability to speak and make new friends.

Leo - Archangel Michael

Michael the Archangel is the chief of the heavenly armies and protects the sign of Leo. His name means the one who is like God, and he is the symbol of justice. He is considered the greatest of all the Archangels.

Archangel Michael collaborates with the Blue Ray and rules the day on Sunday. Michael helps with communication and is known as the Prince of Archangels.

Leo is a sign that has excellent organizational skills, and they are always willing to fight to succeed. They are competitive and loyal to their loved ones.

Archangel Michael helps you to be aware of your thoughts and feelings and encourages you to act. Michael offers you protection, self-confidence, strength, and unconditional love.

Archangel Michael is charged with freeing us from fear, negativity, dramas, and intimidation. This Archangel is charged with dismantling all dysfunctional structures, such as corrupt government systems and financial organizations.

Michael is the protector of all humanity; you can call on him to strengthen you to change direction and find your purpose. Call Michael if you feel a lack of motivation.

This Archangel works for cooperation and harmony with others, and specializes in removing energetic implants, and cutting the ties that paralyze us.

Michael helps us to stand up for our truths without compromising our principles, he brings peace and when we are ready to discard old concepts and beliefs, Archangel Michael supports us by cutting the ties that bind us negatively and prevent us from developing our potential.

Archangel Michael guides those who feel stuck in their profession and helps us to discover the light within us by giving us courage when we face tricky situations.

Ask Archangel Michael to cut the energetic cords that bind you to situations, toxic people, behavioral patterns, and harmful emotions.

People who connect with Archangel Michael are powerful, strong, and empathetic. Invoke Archangel Michael to protect your home and family, he always comes when we need strength to overcome a challenging conflict.

You can visit their temples during meditation, or sleep, in the etheric realm above the Canadian Rockies.

Virgo - Archangel Raphael

Archangel Raphael protects the sign of Virgo and rules the day on Wednesday. He is one of the main Angels of healing and offers his attributes of efficiency and analytical mentality to the sixth sign of the zodiac.

Virgo is always attentive to details because they like to examine all options before deciding. Sometimes they are shy and do not like to draw attention to themselves.

Archangel Raphael rules Ray #4, the green ray, and is known as the head of the Guardian Angels. He helps develop intuition and helps us open our hearts to the healing powers of the Universe.

Raphael puts you in touch with your spirituality and allows you to find healing in the universal energies. He is known as the physician of the angelic realm as he can direct his healing powers towards the dissolution of negative blockages, and illnesses.

Raphael can be called upon to heal we, and to heal others. Raphael helps to heal relationships and remove addictions. He supports light workers and

and guides us to make positive changes in life.

To invoke him, light green candles. You can visit his temples during meditation or sleep on the etheric plane above Fatima, Portugal.

Libra - Archangel Haniel

Libra is a sign protected by the Archangel Haniel, rules the planet Venus, and the day Friday.

Libra is an impartial sign that always seeks balance between soul, mind, and spirit. They are diplomatic, stable, and balanced. Diplomacy is their most outstanding characteristic as they can see both sides of a conflict, but they are a bit paralyzed when making decisions.

The meaning of the Archangel Haniel is the glory of God, and he connects with us through dreams. He offers us protection, and harmony. Haniel assists us in positive changes, new beginnings, and fosters balance in transitions.

Haniel rules peace, brings inspiration and helps to heal envy and jealousy.

Archangel Haniel motivates us to live in the present moment and to see the reality within ourselves. He encourages us to take care of ourselves and reminds us that we are responsible for being mentally and spiritually healthy. He has the power to transform sadness into happiness and encourages us to respect our own natural rhythms.

Invoke Archangel Haniel to find balance, make your intentions come true and release negative energies. He will help you stay calm during notable events by strengthening your confidence. Haniel empowers spiritual gifts and psychic abilities and reminds us that we are divine beings. He is a warrior Angel, turn to him when you need spiritual support or when you feel emotionally weak, he will give you determination, and the energy to trust your intuition.

Scorpion - Archangel Chamuel and Azrael

Scorpio is protected by the Archangels Azrael and Chamuel. Azrael is an Angel who rules the planet Pluto and Chamuel rules the planet Mars and Tuesday.

Those under the influence of Scorpio are given powerful and intense personalities.

Scorpio has a paranoid personality and is obsessed with what is going on in their lives. They cling tightly to what is theirs and refuse to give in without a fight.

The Archangel Azrael's name means whom God helps, he rules Ray #2 which contains vibrations of love and wisdom. Azrael is often referred to as the Angel of Death and that name reminds us that death is transformation.

Archangel Azrael's purpose is to help those who are in transition from physical life to spiritual life. He possesses much compassion and wisdom and has universal healing energies, for those who are grieving the loss of a loved one.

Archangel Azrael comforts people before their physical death and ensures that they do not suffer during their death, surrounding bereaved family and friends with healing energies.

Invoke Archangel Azrael to comfort a loved one and convey messages of love to the spiritual realm. Azrael can help you go through the stages of grief with acceptance.

Azrael helps to create space in our lives for new energies to come in.

Sagittarius - Archangel Zadkiel

Sagittarius is protected by the Archangel Zadkiel, who works with the Violet Ray, rules the planet Jupiter, and on Thursday.

Sagittarius is optimistic and intuitive by nature, but sometimes they cross the boundaries of reality.

Zadkiel's name means the righteousness of God, but it is also related to darkness, inertia. It helps us to discover the divine aspects within us and to develop skills that serve our life's purposes.

Zadkiel is the Archangel of freedom and forgiveness, he assists in spiritual awakening, bestows blessings, and gifts you with discernment. Use the Violet Flame to invoke the Archangel Zadkiel, it will help you to meditate, and develop your intuition. Zadkiel can be invoked to bring forgiveness to others. He leads the Angels of Mercy and can help you to be tolerant and diplomatic.

The healing energies of Archangel Zadkiel and his Angels of Joy will always help you transform memories, break through limitations, erase energetic blockages, and get rid of addictions. Zadkiel encourages you to love and forgive without fear and reminds you to love yourself, and others, unconditionally.

The Archangel Zadkiel is the energetic source behind poverty and wealth and all their manifestations, so he is associated with luck and chance. Zadkiel reminds you that good and bad luck are earned by each individual person, and he values fortune accordingly.

Archangel Zadkiel is responsible for the beginnings and endings of things; he can be called upon to bring an end to a painful situation. Archangel Zadkiel helps us find the inner courage to do the right thing for ourselves, and for others.

To connect with Archangel Zadkiel, use violet-colored candles, or amethyst quartz. Archangel Zadkiel is associated with the Ascended Master Saint Germain, and protects mystics,

Archangel Zadkiel and Saint Amethyst have their etheric retreat, called the Temple of Purification on the island of Cuba.

Zadkiel heals emotional wounds and painful memories, increases your self-esteem, and helps you develop your natural talents and skills.

If you want more tolerance in conflicting situations, turn to Archangel Zadkiel, he will transmute everything dark and raise your vibration.

Capricorn - Archangel Uriel

Capricorn is protected by the Archangel Uriel. This Archangel means Fire of God, rules the Red Ray, and is associated with light, lightning, and thunder.

Uriel can show us how we can heal our lives, help us to understand the concept of karma, and to understand why things are the way they are. Uriel relates to divine magic, problem solving, spiritual understanding, and helps us realize our potential.

Uriel should be invoked when you are working with issues related to economics and politics. You can also invoke him for greater intuition.

Uriel helps you release your fears and opens the channels for divine communication, promotes peace, helps release our obsessive behavior patterns and brings practical solutions.

Uriel can be called upon for intellectual work, and to recognize the light within us.

Archangel Uriel has his etheric retreat in the Tatra Mountains in Poland, and you can ask to be taken there to have your fears healed.

Aquarius - Archangel Uriel

Aquarius is protected by the Archangel Uriel, giving this sign a humanitarian character.

Uriel works with the Ruby Ray and rules the planet Uranus.

Aquarius is independent, and progressive. Archangel Uriel helps with problem solving and finding solutions and is one of the most powerful Archangels.

Uriel helps to release energy blockages in the body, and since he is known as the Angel of Salvation, he can show us how we can heal our lives, finding blessings in adversity, turning defeats into victories, and releasing painful burdens.

Uriel is the Angel of transformation, creativity, and divine order, he rules the missionaries, and is the guardian of the writers. He is the interpreter of prophecies, and of our dreams. He impels us to take responsibility for our lives and brings transforming energies to our minds.

Archangel Uriel is invoked for clarity and intuition. He works to develop in us the qualities of mercy and compassion.

He offers protection, teaches selfless service, and promotes cooperation.

The Archangel Uriel clears old fears and replaces them with wisdom, propitiates vital enlightenment for those who feel they have lost their way and who have emotions related to abandonment and suicide.

Archangel Uriel works to eradicate fear and restore hope, and always seeks to protect the welfare of people who are unable to exercise their free will.

Call upon Archangel Uriel to help you develop your full potential and protect you from envy.

You can ask to visit his temples during your meditation sessions or in your dreams.

Archangel Uriel has his etheric retreat in the Tatra Mountains in Poland.

Pisces - Archangel Azrael and Zadkiel

The sign of Pisces is protected and supervised by the Archangel Azrael and the Archangel Zadkiel.

Archangel Azrael rules the planet Neptune and Archangel Zadkiel rules the planet Jupiter and Thursday. Zadkiel works in the Violet Ray.

Pisces tend to be idealistic, and sensitive; they love to be in love. Every aspect of life should have some romance in it.

Archangel Zadkiel is the guardian of the Violet Flame, which has a super high vibratory frequency.

Archangel Zadkiel is known as the Angel of Understanding and Compassion and is related to darkness, contemplation, and nurturing.

Zadkiel is on a mission to help you with spiritual awakening, he bestows blessings that are designed through faith to increase understanding.

Using the Violet Flame, Archangel Zadkiel helps you to meditate, and increases your psychic abilities. Zadkiel helps open our minds and gives us psychic protection.

Zadkiel encourages tolerance and helps people to love themselves and connects us to our soul's mission.

Archangel Zadkiel brings healing to our emotional wounds, frees us, and motivates people to show mercy to others.

Working with Zadkiel increases your self-esteem and helps you remember and develop your natural talents, skills, and abilities. Call Zadkiel if you need help remembering specific details and facts.

Call upon Archangel Zadkiel to help you heal and transcend your negative emotions and improve your mental functions.

The Archangel Zadkiel is the energy behind poverty and wealth, and all their manifestations, so he is related to chance. Zadkiel imparts justice without prejudice, but is merciful to those who deserve it, he is responsible for beginnings and endings, and you can call on him whenever you want to end a chaotic circumstance.

Archangel Zadkiel can break through blocked or stagnant energies caused by anger and guilt.

Zadkiel and the Holy Amethyst have their etheric sanctuary on the island of Cuba.

Angel protector of your Zodiac Sign

Many times, we feel alone, without physical and emotional protection. Even if you cannot see it, your guardian Angel or spiritual guides are always with you, since the day you were born, protecting you. Invoke the name of your Angel in the moments when you feel you need help or advice, choose to put your life in their hands and they will lead you on the best path.

Aries. Angel Anauel

This Angel confers to the sign Aries an indestructible health and protection against the dark forces of evil, among them envy. Aries has an inflexible personality, they get desperate and angry very quickly, but their compassion and susceptibility opens all doors for them. This Guardian Angel is also known as Haniel, or Ariel. It is the Angel of creativity and sensuality. He arranges the success in couples, love and prevents the sufferings of the heart.

Taurus. Angel Uriel

Uriel *will always come into your life when you need him for exams, medical studies, and when you have separation problems. Uriel will always protect your spirit and enlighten your mind so you can make the right decisions.*

Gemini. Angel Eyael

Eyael *will always protect you from adversities and free you from injustices, especially in the place where you work. This Angel is incredibly special of him, he knows with whom it is good for you to relate, that is, he will make you surround yourself with influential people who will help you succeed. This Angel encourages you to always look at the positive side of things and encourages your feelings of generosity and desire to help others.*

Cancer. Angel Rochel

Rochel *endows the Cancer sign with excellent vision to detect dangers, as well as creativity and talents to discover hidden secrets. He will destroy all your fears and your enemies. ask him to give you clarity, shrewdness and cunning.*

Leo. Angel Nelkhael

Nelkhael will keep sadness and low self-esteem away from you. He will guard you from people who slander you out of envy and will help you to keep your commitments and assume your responsibilities. The problems of your daily life will be easier to cope with under his influence. Nelkhael offers you support in your darkest and saddest moments.

Virgo. Angel Melahel

Melahel when invoked will drive away violence from your life and your environment. This Angel will provide an energy that will drive back your enemies or make you invisible. He is also related to harmony and healing. He will bring you ways to connect with the universe and enjoy the secrets of nature.

Libra. Angel Yerathel

Yerathel *offers the sign of Libra a lot of intelligence and insight to be able to detect your enemies. This Angel provides you with lucidity and reflective capacity, characteristics that will allow you to surround yourself with the right people. Yerathel gives you the weapons of justice and allows you to be wise and tolerant. By invoking Yerathel, you will achieve success.*

Scorpion. Angel Azrael

Azrael, known as the Archangel of death, will rescue you from injustice and at the same time renew your image and hopes. He reminds you that the universe loves you, he will guide you on the path of love, tenderness, and harmony at home. If you want to meet the right partner to create a lasting relationship and start a family, invoke this, Angel.

Sagittarius. Umabel Angel

Umabel repels envy from your relationships, and feelings that can harm you such as anger, jealousy, and hatred. He gives you the eloquence necessary for a calm and distinct expression. He gives you the art of persuasion. You know how to tip the scales in your favor, improve your communication skills so you know how to explain important things. He helps you make the right decisions, at the right time.

Capricorn. Angel Sitael

Sitael, build shields around you, organize your life, and if you do not know which path to take, think about it and you will instantly focus. If you wish to improve your economic situation, cure yourself of an illness, or move, change, invoke this Angel and wait for the miracle.

Aquarius. Angel Gabriel

Gabriel will fight day by day, so that you can fight your battles. If you want help because there are people who want to harm you or put you in danger, ask this Angel for protection. If you are afraid that someone will commit an injustice against you, by invoking this Angel you will surely neutralize your enemy.

Pisces. Angel Daniel

Daniel will always keep you safe from illness and physical pain, you will always come out of all the mishaps and accidents that come your way.

Angelic Numbers and their Meanings

We are evolving spiritually, and every day the numerical sequences are seen by more people. These messages that come from a higher source, that is, from our Angels or spiritual guides, have the purpose of guiding you.

The Angels want to get our attention and communicate with us through these numbers in sequence. This is how they help us heal our lives. Unfortunately, some ignore these signs thinking they are coincidences when it is synchronicity.

Your Angels send you messages through number sequences, they may very subtly whisper in your ear so that you look at a specific place and notice the time on the clock, or the number on an advertisement. They show you meaningful number sequences in a physical way, by placing a car in front of you when you are standing in traffic that has a specific license plate number.

When you notice a numerical sequence repeating itself, ask the Angels what they are trying to tell you, and you will find that they will give you the information you need. Watch your thoughts jealously and be sure to think only of what you want, not what you do not want.

Numbers in sequence have a specific meaning, these numbers have messages in three dimensions, and guide us in our lives.

When you learn to interpret these numbers, you will feel more connected to the Angels, and this connection is the key that will open the door to peace, hope, and love.

Each number has vibrations that relate directly to their meanings and the Angels draw our attention to these number sequences because they feel devotion, and love for us. When you notice a number sequence, try to listen to what your Angel wants you to do or know.

The more you see these signs, the more frequently they will appear in your life. When you understand the meanings of these numbers and accept that they are not coincidences, but important, purposeful messages, you will learn to communicate with your Angels.

These number sequences can be birth dates, anniversaries, phone numbers or car license plates, and are a subtle reminder that something magical is happening in your life. It is up to you to go within, listen to your intuition and find out what the messages are telling you and what they mean to you.

How to Read Angelic Numbers

Numbers surround us in our daily lives, and when we recognize and interpret these numerical sequences, we can feel more connected to our Angels. This connection allows us to create a powerful connection with the angelic realm.

Interpreting these numerical sequences is an effective way to receive messages from your guardian angels and spirit guides. You should always use your intuitive abilities.

Important Angel Numbers in 2024

111: *You should take a less enthusiastic approach to life and count your blessings.*

222: *You must remain true to your spiritual beliefs.*

333: *Learn to express your feelings.*

444: *You are at a crossroads, and you must embrace spirituality.*

555: *A personal evolution or physical change awaits you.*

666: *You are stuck in your past and need to let it go to succeed.*

777: Your Angels want to applaud you, praise you and encourage you to keep going the way you are going.

888: The universe supports your path and wants you to have many successes.

808: Your Angels want you to explore new talents and open yourself to opportunities.

818: Overcome your limits, you are stronger than you think.

999: You are about to begin a new chapter in your life.

1155: Use your personal freedom to become a better person.

1221: Be optimistic and move forward. Great triumphs await you.

1144: If you want something, be brave and pursue your dreams.

See your birthday frequently.
When you see your birth date numbers very often, it indicates that you should focus on finding your purpose in life, and your soul's mission. Seeing your birthday reminds

you of why you were born and your reason for being on planet Earth at this time.

The Order of Numbers in a Number Sequence

The order of the numbers in a sequence has meaning. If you see that there are three digits in a sequence, the middle number is the focus, as it represents the key to the message,

Each number must be analyzed independently, then all the digits must be added together until they are reduced to one.

***Example**: a number sequence of 172 can be interpreted in diverse ways. The number 7 must be interpreted first. Then each number individually 1, 7 and then 2. The whole number 172 must be added up and reduced to a single digit 1 + 7 + 2 = 10 (1 + 0 = 1). This makes the number 1 the most relevant message in this numerical sequence. Remember to always use your intuition and you to decipher the message, it does not matter if you do not understand the message from a human point of view, your subconscious mind understands.*

Numerical Sequence. Repetition of 0

The number 0 is related to meditation. The starting point, the totality, and the continuous cycles. Or it is the Alpha and the Omega.

The number 0 encloses the attributes of all numbers. Alpha is the beginning and Omega is the end. All numbers with 0 bring you closer to the universal energy.

The number 0, if repeated, its message is related to spiritual aspects, since 0 represents the beginning of a spiritual journey and the uncertainties that may occur. When 0 is repeated, it asks you to listen to your intuition, that is where you will find all the answers.

Sequence 00 *relates to meditation. The Universe is emphasizing that you pay attention.*

The 000 sequence *wants you to make sure that your thoughts, and desires are of a positive nature, as this is what you will attract into your life.*

The sequence 0000 *indicates that a situation or problem has end.*

When combined with another number the potential of the number 0 is magnified and stimulates the energies and vibrations of the number with which it is being combined.

Number Sequence. Repetition of 1

The number 1 has the vibrations of new beginnings, individuality, success, strength, and creativity.

The number 1 is the number where all manifestation begins. It is the energy that initiates all actions and is the number of new projects, courage, and the desire for expansion on all levels.

All numbers are divisible by 1. We are all one, therefore, we are all connected. When Angel Number 1 appears, it is a message to analyze your thoughts and focus on your desires with a positive mindset.

Angel Number 1 speaks of changes and new actions that will require determination so that the goal can be achieved. It means that an energetic door has opened, and this will quickly manifest your thoughts into reality. You must choose your thoughts making sure they match your desires. Do not focus on fears as you may manifest them in your life.

The number 11 is a master number and relates to our soul's mission. The essence of the message of this number sequence is to develop your intuition, and metaphysical faculties. The number 11 represents the beginning of your spiritual enlightenment. If the number 11 appears repeatedly, your Angels are asking you to pay attention to your repetitive thoughts and ideas.

*When the **numerical sequence 111** appears, you should monitor your thoughts carefully and make sure to think only about what you really want.*

The sequence of 1111 appears to many people and is a sign that there is an opportunity opening for you, and your thoughts are manifesting at the speed of light. The 1111 means that the Universe has just taken a snapshot of your thoughts and is manifesting your ideas in material form.

Number Sequence. Repetition of 2
The number 2 is related to the energies of peace, diplomacy, justice, altruism, and harmony.

The number 2 is the vibration of balance, intuition, and emotion. It is the number of tolerances, and if you see it often it means that you must have faith, trust, and courage as your requests manifest. Patience is necessary, but all will be well.

The essence of the master number 22 is the potential to master all areas: spiritual, physical, emotional, and mental. The number 22 is about balance, and new opportunities.

When Angel Number 22 repeats in your life, it asks you to have a balanced, peaceful stance in all areas of your life. The message is to keep your faith.

*The message of **Angel Number 222** is that everything will turn out well overall, so you should not put your energies into negative things.*

***The numerical sequence 2222** indicates you must continue to maintain your positive thoughts by positively affirming and visualizing. Rewards are on the way.*

Number Sequence. Repetition of 3
***The number 3** relates to vibrations and energies of freedom, inspiration, creativity, growth, intelligence, and sensitivity.*

The number 3 signifies that an outpouring of energy is in action and represents abundance on the physical, emotional, mental, financial, and spiritual levels.

*When **Angel Number 3** appears very often it means that the Ascended masters are close to you. They have answered your prayers and wish to help you in your soul's mission.*

***The number 33** is a Master Number, and its message is that anything is possible. If you happen to be considering a major change in your life, Number 33 says that if its purpose and your intentions are of a positive nature, your desires will manifest.*

***The 333 number sequence** sends you a message that you must have faith in humanity. The Ascended masters are working on all levels, and they protect you. They will guide you on your path.*

***The numerical sequence of 3333** indicates that the Ascended master's and Angels are close to you at that time, they are aware of your situation and know the best way to do things. They will help you.*

Number Sequence. Repetition of 4

The number 4 *relates to energies of hard work, practicality, productivity, and loyalty.*

The number 4 *represents the four elements: Air, Fire, Water and Earth, and the four cardinal points: north, south, east, and west. It symbolizes the principle of putting ideas into form and when it indicates that your Angels are around you. The Angels offer you support and strength so that you can do the necessary work. They understand that you are working towards your goals and will help you.*

The numerical sequence 44 *indicates that the Angels are supporting you and that you have a strong connection with the angelic realm.*

The message of the **Angelic Number 444** *sequence is that you have nothing to fear because everything is as it should be, and everything is super fine. The things you have been working on will be successful. The repetition of 444 indicates that you are surrounded by supportive Angels.*

The angelic numerical sequence 4444 *indicates that you are surrounded by Angels who are watching over you and supporting you in your daily life. They encourage you to keep working to achieve your goals. The 4444 is a message that the help you need is nearby.*

Number Sequence. Repetition of 5
The number 5 *relates to attributes of personal freedom, individualism, life changes, and life lessons learned.*

When **Angel Number 5** *appears, it indicates that there are changes in your life that are coming but they will be for the better. Energies are building up to force changes that are needed, these changes will come unexpectedly, but they will bring positive opportunities that will push you in the right direction.*

The numerical sequence of 55 *is a message from your Angels that it is time to free yourself from the restrictions that have held you back in the past. It is time to live. The Number 55 heralds' profound changes ahead, if they are not already all around you.*

The 555 number sequence indicates *that monumental changes await you in your life. Number 555 tells you that these significant transformations are here and that you can discover the amazing life you deserve as a spiritual being.*

The numerical sequence of 5555 *is a message that your life is about to go through major changes,*

Number Sequence. Repetition of 6

The number 6 *symbolizes integrity, peace, altruism, and growth.*

When Angel Number 6 appears repeatedly it speaks of our ability to use our intellect to achieve positive results. When the number 6 appears, your Angels are telling you to balance your thoughts, to free yourself from doubts or worries about financial matters.

Angel Number 66 *is a message to trust the Universe and your Angels that your wishes regarding your family and social life will be fulfilled. The repetition of the number 66 tells you to keep your thoughts focused on achieving your goals.*

The numerical sequence of 666 *indicates that it is time to concentrate on your spirituality to heal any problems in your life. The number 666 asks you to be receptive to receive and accept the help you need. The Angel's number 666 can also indicate that your thoughts are out of balance.*

The numerical sequence 6666 *one indicates that your thoughts are out of balance, and that you are focused on the material aspects of life. Prosperity energies are being diverted and your anxiety is a barrier.*

Angel Number 6666 asks you to balance your thoughts between the spiritual and the material, to keep faith and trust that your material and emotional needs will be met.

Number Sequence. Repetition of 7

The number 7 relates to energies of spirituality, wisdom, and inner wisdom.

The number 7 is a mystical number that symbolizes humanity's deep inner need for spiritual connection.

Angel Number 7 indicates that you are on the right path and that you will find that things will flow freely to you. Your job is to maintain your enthusiasm.

The repetition of the 7 speaks of a beneficial time to be successful and self-controlled and indicates that your ambitions can be realized, and challenges overcome.

The numerical sequence of 77 means you are on the right path. and rewards are coming your way. You must stand firm.

Angel Number 777 notifies you that it is time to reap the rewards of your hard work and efforts. Your wishes will come true. Angel Number 777 is a positive sign.

The 7777 sequence is a message from your Angels that you are on the right path and your dreams and desires are manifesting in your life. It is an extremely positive sign and means that there are more miracles on the way for you.

Number Sequence. Repetition of 8
The number 8 is related to energies of wealth, money, power, business, investment, independence, peace, and love for humanity.

Angel Number 8 indicates that financial abundance is on its way into your life. Being the number of karmas, 8 suggests that you will receive rewards.

***The repetition of the number 88** is a message to keep your finances in check and suggests that your hard work will be justly rewarded.*

***The numerical sequence of 888** indicates that your life's purpose is supported by the Universe. The Universe is generous and wants to reward you, so financial prosperity will come into your life. It may also indicate that you are ending a phase in your life.*

The numerical sequence 8888 indicates that there is light at the end of the tunnel and is a message for you to enjoy the fruits of your labor.

Number Sequence. Repetition of 9
The number 9 relates to the vibrations of intelligence, compassion, and intuition.

When the Angelic Number 9 appears, it is a message that your life purpose and soul mission is to give service through your talents, and passions. It indicates the end of a phase or relationship in your life. *The number sequence of 99 is a* message to remember to live a positive and successful life on all levels.

The number 999 indicates that the world needs you to use your talents, you are a Lightworker, and the Angels are asking you to live up to your potential.

The numerical sequence 9999 is a message to people who are ambassadors of light on planet earth to keep their light shining bright.

Angelic Cards for each Zodiac Sign 2024

Aries. Zadquiel Angel Card

Zadquiel *is the Angel of mercy; he symbolizes altruism and personal selflessness in favor of others. Zadquiel will help you to be a compassionate person. He will help you find lost objects, improve your memory, and help you heal physically, emotionally, and mentally. Zadquiel will support you as you learn to forgive yourself and others, remember valuable information and study. If you want to leave behind any prejudice invoke the Archangel Zadquiel*

because one of his main tasks is to help you see your inner light.

You will stop seeing your mistakes as negative aspects of your life and start seeing them to learn. You will also see your flaws as blessings in your life because perfection is impossible to achieve and even in chaos there is beauty.

You will look for ways to focus on becoming the best version of yourself, the best person you can imagine. Archangel Zadquiel is a higher being that you can invoke when you feel frustration, sadness, or negativity. His armies can help you find the positive side of all situations and make you feel better emotionally.

It is time to let go of any guilt you cling to regarding mistakes you may have made in the past. Give yourself credit for doing your best, even if the results were not what you would have liked. Focus on the changes you have made that have made you a better person.

Taurus. Angelic Card Uriel

Uriel, the Angel of the keys warns you to embark on new paths and to beware of bad influences. If you are beginning to doubt yourself, or losing faith, this card reminds you that all things are possible through learning. Knowledge can open all doors, and new skills can open all locks. The flame of knowledge never dies and is within your reach.

Uriel will never lead you down an uncertain path without reason. He is there to support you along your journey, allowing you to speak your truth and become the best version of yourself.

This card reminds you that you are wiser than you think, and your inner wisdom will give you all the answers you seek. Embrace this knowledge and trust it. If you have doubts, ask it to give you obvious signs to validate your ideas.

Uriel helps to illuminate cloudy situations. However, he only illuminates one step at a time, so you may not be able to clearly discern the result of your actions. You must trust because you will know what step to take next, along the way, with Uriel's help.

Never forget that forgiveness can work miracles. When you release the past, a weight is lifted off your shoulders and a sense of freedom comes over you. Ask Uriel to help you relieve sadness or pain caused by others so you can be free.

Gemini. Raphael Angel Card

It represents strength and personal brilliance.

You must harness your personality to achieve success. Raphael's most powerful gift is his ability to transform lives through a cascade of positive energy. You can access this channel of energy through affirmations or meditation techniques. Throughout history, Raphael has had various appearances in many different religions, making him an Archangel accessible to people of all faiths.

Now is not the time to give up on sick relationships. There is still hope for the future.

Substantial changes will come into your life. You may find yourself on a new career path, entering a new relationship, or moving to a new house or city. Embrace these exciting events, Raphael will be by your side all the way.

Remember, the future is always changing. If you do not like the outcome, this is your opportunity to make changes that will alter it. If you like this outcome, stay on your current path. To maintain your current path, keep doing what you are doing. Take it easy or change the intensity with which you are currently working.

Rafael will help you recognize the ramifications of your actions and your purpose in life.

Cancer. Haniel Angel Card

It represents all the good that the earth offers us. A new successful stage will be presented in your life.

Haniel may be asking you to slow down and really think about the action you plan to take.

Haniel is trying to guide you to a higher choice, so put aside everything you think you know about your current circumstances or situation and simply allow the Universe and Haniel to point the way.

When it is necessary to make a weighty decision, this Angel will send you many signals through synchronicity as to which is the right path to take.

It is important that you take some time to regroup, as this Angel may come to give you the guidance you need at that moment.

This letter has appeared to bring you messages of hope, as well as to indicate that it is time for you to start being more aware of all the messages that the Universe and Haniel are sending you.

You may need some answers to some tough questions, or you may have been wondering if things will ever get better in your life. Haniel has appeared to say that they will, however, think carefully about what you say to others and what they say to you. Haniel will never judge you for anything you think or say, however, he will urge you to focus on those things that bring you a sense of joy, peace, and gratitude.

Leo. Gabriel Angel Card

Gabriel shows you the duality of good and bad. He augurs travel for you,
 You may begin to have some thoughts in your mind that will surprise you. It is important for you to keep in mind that the stronger your emotional reaction to them, the more you should pay attention to them. Notice what others tell you that fits with what you have been thinking. When you ask Gabriel to confirm that what you have been thinking is true, he is always quick to act, so pay attention.

You may feel inclined to spend time meditating or reading self-help books. Gabriel is encouraging you to do so, because he knows how important it is to fill your mind with positive thoughts.

Gabriel allows you to understand that as you make changes in your life and face challenges, you are in complete safety. He knows what will be best for you. Remember that when you are asked to wait, it means that you have something better than you could ever imagine, prepared just for you. That is why you must accept the situation.

Do not rush when you see something that may break your will. The next door will open when the time comes, and you will have new strength.

Virgo. Remiel Angel Card

Remiel represents the mercy of God showing that something has been hidden from you. During this year 2024 it is important to dedicate yourself to acquiring new knowledge, ideas, and skills. You will want to start learning and this card encourages you to follow this desire.

If you are currently studying, Remiel asks you to continue your education. Sometimes, in the process of acquiring new knowledge and skills, we have a desire to quickly evaluate them in practice, and this leads to the fact that many people drop out of school early.

This card advises you not to rush things. Continue your education. The personal growth that accompanies learning can bring you joy.

Remiel knows that you have many responsibilities in life, so you need time, money, and other resources. This card wants to remind you that regular doses of entertainment can help you achieve your goals. Have fun and laugh, relax. In this state, you become more receptive to innovative ideas, spiritual links, teachings, and divine energy.

In addition, your cheerfulness attracts to you many wonderful people who can help you. Your cheerful outlook toward the world opens new opportunities for you.

Libra. St. Michael Angel Card

Archangel Michael represents justice, and the forces of good prevailing over evil. You do not have to forgive mistakes, but if you forgive a person, you will find peace. You have many negative emotions and Michael calls you to cleanse your soul, he understands that these feelings can be completely justified, but he asks you to see the high price you are paying for accumulating all this anger.

Get rid of all the pain and anger of the past. When you forgive yourself and others, your karma is cleansed of the *burden of past mistakes. All the power of the creator is within you. All the power of divine love and wisdom is at your disposal. You can see the angels and the future, and you also have the intelligence to know the universal wisdom of the divine mind.*

Thanks to your emotional power, you will be able to confront other people and your psychic power will be truly infinite during 2024. The angels ask you to eliminate all fears associated with the use of force. They see your true power radiating from Divine Love. Allow yourself to shine with this love so that your true power can accomplish the miracles you need. Sometimes you may think that you are a hostage to life's circumstances, but this card asks you to understand that you are your own prisoner. Once you know you can break free, you will be free immediately.

Everything you do in your life; you do by your choice. Even prisoners are free to choose their thoughts, and, therefore, can find peace and happiness under any circumstances. The next time you start a sentence with the words "I am forced...", stop. Ask Michael to show you alternatives. He will help you.

Scorpion. Raziel Angelic Card

He is the Angel of secrets and mysteries. He will reveal to you in 2024 mysteries of the earthly and spiritual realm.

A period of spiritual growth begins in your life this year, and although you will experience mixed feelings of confusion, fear, and surprises, you must not lose your cool. Discard your fears. Raziel supports you, loves you and guides you every second. Do not worry about how your future will harmonize with your growth.

You will get important messages in your dreams. There is a time of wonderful changes in your life, so trust Raziel, he will take care of exactly what you want.

Changes in your life can be painful if you do not show flexibility in your thoughts. If you have a new love, remember that the past remains in the past, away from the new happiness.

You need to expand your horizons, and Raziel is here to help you. It is time to listen to your heart. Be aware of the importance of tact and do not be too stubborn. Trust yourself. Do not worry. Whatever challenge you face, you are on your way to serenity.

You need comfort and this angel gives you faith. Soon you may be on the road to the happiness and harmony you need. Do charitable deeds, it will help you feel better, and you will receive good things in return.

Sagittarius. Metatron Angel Card

It represents the greatness and strength that a person should have. By inviting Metatron into your life, you open yourself to receive spiritual and energetic healing, to cleanse yourself of all negativities. You get protection from illness and, of course, you get closer to transformation.

You need to honor all the emotions you are feeling right now whether they are good or bad. Emotions can teach us a lot about our true feelings and the people or situations that evoked them.

You may be getting feedback from other people, and this is the mirror for you to see what is inside.

Metatron protects you by cutting the cords that bind you to people, places, and things. If you are afraid, lack courage or need protection, imagine his protective mantle around you, helping you to live your truth. This is a special card. You are guided and sustained. Metatron is with you currently, and there is a special message he wants to share with you. Close your eyes, take a few deep breaths, go deep within, and relax. Listen to the advice you receive.

You are perfect, and that is a spiritual fact. Metatron gently embraces you and lets you know that you are the perfect spiritual being. You are not alone, no matter how you feel. Place all your worries in his hands and allow him to heal your problems through divine guidance.

Your life has meaning, and every step is an essential part of your journey, but rest assured that you are always protected and that all the angels are watching you with great love. Trust.

Capricorn. Raguel Angel Card

He is the Angel who gives advice to men to guide them on their path in life.

Your soul mate will come into your life. If you are free, consider the card as a sign from Raguel that your soul mate is present.

Suppose you are currently in a relationship, and you know that it is not your soul mate. In that case, you and your partner will be gently guided to improve the relationship, *or to a graceful end, to obtain a new relationship with your soul mate.*

Focusing better on your heart's desires and better contact with your higher self will help you complete all the troublesome work and issues you have put off. You have a list of goals for this year 2024 you should clear your mind and focus your thoughts better on what you really want, and you will be able to achieve your desires.

Visualizing your wishes is the fastest way to open the door to the universe and its offer to fulfill them. Do not worry about how your wishes will come to you. Leave it in the hands of the universe.

Listen to your higher self and ask the angels to guide you. Start acting as soon as you feel encouraged. Sometimes the results may not be what you expected, but that is the beauty of life and the universe. You are guided to what you really need.

Aquarius. Amiel Angel Card

It heralds changes you will have to adapt to and unexplored terrain you will visit.

Allow yourself to spend quality time with your family and friends. You can draw a lot of strength from those who love you. If you have a problem with a family member or friend, Amiel encourages you to bring it to the surface.

Releasing and healing will set you free, which will create more favorable opportunities for you. Or a simple act of spending quality time with your loved ones will yield positive results.

As you advance spiritually, you will become more sensitive to the dense, negative vibrations of reality along with the higher dimensions of love. This card is an encouragement to clear your energetic space.

This year take a relaxed breath and imagine that you are surrounded by an orb of white light. Amiel brings you blessings.

Your prayers will be heard and answered. Love, finances, friendship, and family will be determined by your attitude. Ask Amiel to help you treat yourself with the respect you so richly deserve. When you are in this state of self-esteem, you are full of positive energy that overflows to the people around you. This enables you to attract positive and loving relationships that are fulfilling.

Pisces. Dobiel Angel Card

Messenger of divine secrets.

Whether angels, family, neighbors, or friends, you will receive help. By asking for help, you are allowing the universe to act on your behalf. Believe that you will be led to the right person or situation that can help you in any matter.

We are not islands unto ourselves, and we are not obligated to solve all problems independently. Angels love to share, and a shared problem is half the problem. Never be afraid to ask for help. Miracles exist and you are entitled to them.

You must encourage yourself to stay positive and focus only on what you want. Thinking about what you do not want only maintains negative results. Even a small amount of focus on positive thoughts can change your life for the better.

If you feel that you lack a positive approach, ask the universe for help and, most importantly, believe that it will help you. Even this small act alone will help make a noticeable difference in your life.

You have the skills, confidence, and knowledge to have a successful business. That for which are you waiting? With this card, Dobiel wants to tell you that you have the talent to succeed in your own business. If you thought you would become independent and start working on your own this year 2024, this card is a good sign that your intuition is right. Sometimes it is difficult to take the first step, rest assured that Dobiel is guiding you in this matter and trust him.

Meaning of 2024

2024 is the perfect number to create. In fact, its vibration is connected to a vast realm of infinite possibilities.

This vibration can take different forms. It can be about shaping your future, or painting in your mind the image of what your life will be like when your deepest desires come true. This will give you the motivation you need to move forward in your life.

2024 is a powerful year because your psychic senses will be amplified. If you have desires to have more intuition or open your perception, this is the perfect year to do so. This is the perfect time to create in the literal sense of the word. In fact, it is a highly creative angelic number.

Angelic Colors for Physical and Spiritual Healing during the Year 2024

The colors that surround us, and the ones we choose to decorate our lives have meaning, and specific vibrations that influence us in diverse ways.

All colors influence our moods and feelings. That is why colors have been used to treat illnesses, for protection, to attract a soul mate, and to uplift the spirit.

The effect of colors on the human mind, and the ability to use them to express emotions and situations has been used since prehistoric times. For that reason, the importance of colors is fundamental for the continuation of our species and survival.

The meaning of colors can be expressed on an emotional and spiritual level. On an emotional level we feel the influence of color on the nervous system. Assorted colors evoke different feelings. Colors can induce action, calm, anxiety, or tranquility, so our moods are influenced by the colors we choose for our clothes and our environment.

Aries. Green Color 2024

Green is a color used for healing, as it generates well-being. It is considered the optimal color for healing, stimulates growth, vital force, balances the body and mind, and strengthens. Green is rejuvenating and anti-inflammatory. It aids memory, relieves paranoia and nervous exhaustion.

Green has a palliative effect on the nervous system, calms irritations and relieves pain. Physically, it is linked to the muscles, bones, and lungs. It is good for treating problems connected to the heart and circulatory system. It balances blood pressure.

Green is healing for feelings of remorse, and for overcoming any limiting emotions. Green energy is healing for insecurity and feelings of inadequacy.

Green helps to overcome obstacles and change direction, stimulates the pituitary gland and is effective in relieving emotional imbalances. It can be used to counteract panic attacks and addictions.

Taurus. Brown Color 2024

Brown helps to control hyperactivity, hypertension, and anxiety, as it is restorative. Brown can also help relieve *painful situations, both physical and emotional, as it has a stabilizing effect and provides a sense of healing. It facilitates connection with the Earth and gives a sense of order.*

Brown helps with the stability of all body systems and the immune system.

Gemini. Yellow Color 2024

Yellow is used to reduce depression, as it awakens feelings of joy and happiness.

Yellow stimulates the mind and nervous system, activates memory and communication. It is related to the liver, stomach, thyroid, tubes, large and small intestines.

Yellow is used to control the adrenal glands, gall bladder, liver, and stomach.

Yellow can be used to treat psychological problems such as depression, and melancholy. This color helps a weak memory and can be used to treat psychic exhaustion. It can work on fear and gradually release tension. This color is related to self-esteem, ego, courage, and self-confidence.

Cancer Red Color 2024

Red is used to treat paralyzing conditions and to stimulate vital energy. It is revitalizing and helps to overcome depression and melancholy. It is a help for those who are afraid of life.

This color is related to the adrenal glands and the senses of hearing, smell, taste, sight, and touch. Red is linked to the circulatory system, the heart, sexual organs, and the bladder. Red causes hemoglobin to increase and raises body temperature.

This color is beneficial for states of weakness, to treat arthritis, muscular pains, and bacterial diseases, it also stimulates the metabolism.

If you are someone who tends to live in the past, red helps you become rooted in the moment.

Leo. Pink Color 2024

Pink has beneficial healing properties, but it is also the color of unconditional love.

This color can increase blood pressure, heartbeat, and pulse, it also stimulates and confidence.

It helps restore youthfulness, is used to treat conditions related to lack of self-love, feelings of loneliness and serves to alleviate jealousy. It can also be used to calm emotional and mental problems, is very relaxing and promotes feelings of contentment.

Virgo. Gray Color 2024
The color gray is excellent for mental and physical cleansing. Gray draws negative energy from the body and replaces it with positive energies.

It is the color of intellect, and inner wisdom. It encourages and enhances patience and perseverance. Gray is perceived as a classic and elegant color. It is the color of dignity and authority.

Libra. Blue Color 2024
Blue symbolizes calmness and peace of mind. It is a color that elevates consciousness and connection with the angelic realms.

This color lowers blood pressure calms the nervous system and is anti-inflammatory. It brings tranquility, peace of mind and reduces pain.

It is sleeping regulating, relaxing, and refreshing and brings mental clarity. Blue represents inspiration and spiritual expansion.

Golden Scorpion Color 2024

Gold is a healing and transforming color.

In color therapy it is used to overcome addictions, and it is antidepressant, as it is inspirational.

Gold is related to confidence and self-esteem, creativity, abundance, and prosperity.

Sagittarius. Orange Color 2024
courage and vitality

The healing energies of orange stimulate inner awareness. In therapy orange is used to revitalize energies. It is used for emotional ailments and to help depressive states as it awakens joy, and interest in life. It can dispel lack of confidence and has an antispasmodic effect on the human body.

It is used to treat asthma, bronchitis, and other respiratory problems. It also helps maintain good vision and strengthens the immune system.

Orange strengthens the etheric body and promotes general health.

Capricorn. Magenta Color 2024

Magenta is a color that is related to healing abilities. In therapy it is the color of healing and is used to treat problems related to the brain, and to calm feelings of frustration.

This color can be used to negotiate calm and peace between those who disagree.

Magenta is related to strong but controlled passions; it is a color that encourages boldness.

This color represents compassion and kindness and is the color of emotional balance and universal harmony.

It is the color of change and transformation and helps you to release old patterns of behavior that impede your personal and spiritual development, it encourages us to take responsibility for creating our own realities.

Aquarium. White Color 2024

The color white attunes us to a higher spiritual frequency and divine love. It helps mental clarity and encourages us to remove obstacles.

It has cleansing properties, helps to think clearly and reveal truths. It is a healing color and has the power of transformation.

In therapy, the color white is used to stimulate consciousness and in healing ailments by balancing all spiritual systems.

The vibrations of the color white are the fastest in the spectrum and encompass all colors. It is considered the color of truth, purity, neutrality, peace, and harmony.

Pisces. Silver Color 2024

Silver is a healing color that promotes spiritual growth. It removes negative energies from the body and replaces them with positive ones. It is related to rebirth and reincarnation, and the healing of hormonal imbalances. It is an excellent color for emotional, mental cleansing, as it works on the emotions.

In therapy the silver color is used for hormonal imbalances, and gynecological diseases.

The silver color symbolizes the protective energies, it represents the mystical and mysterious. The silver color helps to eliminate and neutralize dark energies.

Colors of the Archangels and Ascended Masters

Red: *is the first Ray and is related to Archangel Michael, and the Ascended Master El Moria.*

Yellow: *is the second Ray and is related to Archangel Jophiel and Lord Kuthumi.*

Pink: *is the third Ray and is related to the Archangel Chamuel and the Ascended Master Serapis Bey.*

Green: *it is the fourth Ray and is related to the Archangel Gabriel and Paul the Venetian.*

Orange: *it is the fifth Ray and is related to Archangel Raphael and Master Hilary.*

Indigo: *is the sixth Ray and is related to the Archangel Uriel and Jesus Christ.*

Violet: it *is the seventh Ray and is related to the Archangel Zadkiel and Saint-Germain.*

White: *it is related to all the Rays and to the Archangel Gabriel and Paul the Venetian.*

Angelic Predictions by Signs 2024

Aries Predictions

This year 2024 indicates that love, new understanding, and passion await you. Unexpected wealth may come your way, giving you security in your financial life. But remember, you must embrace uncertainty and be open to unexpected changes in your life. You will have achievements and recognition in your professional life.

A bright future awaits you. It is advisable that you look within yourself and take advantage of the qualities you have had since childhood, remember that maturing does not mean abandoning your purest essence, but allowing it to grow with you. You will have the possibility of finding a job that connects better with your interests, and will stimulate your life in many aspects, besides the economic one.

Taurus Predictions

This year 2024 you will also be lucky in the material sphere, but you will have to make efforts to achieve everything you have desired.

You will receive much economic well-being and inner joy. You must be prepared to receive protection in the economic sphere, prosperity will appear in your life in such a way that material inconveniences will disappear. You will start a new life and you will also achieve spiritual abundance.

Some difficulties may arise to solve the problems, so you must be confident and self-confident because everything will be a test that you can overcome.

Your angel recommends that you stay away from conflictive situations and try to neutralize any criticism coming from work colleagues.

Maintain discipline, without neglecting the search for a job that gives you better conditions and a healthier environment. You will end the year with several proposals on the table, remember to ask for divine enlightenment to make the best decisions.

Predictions for Gemini

Love and security come to you this year. You will have a partner with stability and full of happiness.

Love and joy. The light of love is coming into your life, you just must be patient. Enjoy the stability and happiness that is on its way and that you should receive with open arms. Leave behind the feelings of loneliness and receive the pure love that is reserved for you. Your dreams are about to come true. Your wishes may not be fulfilled exactly as you wanted, but eventually the reward will be exactly what you expected.

Your angel warns about situations that can become amplified if you do not pay the necessary attention. Be especially careful of abdominal problems or discomfort, as they could even compromise reproductive organs. Attention in time will keep you in good health.

After a period in which your finances were rocked to the sway of the waves, this year stability will return to your life.

Predictions for Cancer

Do you remember how magical the world around you seemed to be in your childhood? The Angels ask you to restore this magical feeling for yourself by remembering the wonderful powers around you. The Angels really want to support you, to help you discard unnecessary anxiety to radiate joy and spontaneity like a child.

You will protect your freedom above any other value, despite the criticism of others or the possible discussions that may arise in this regard.

It is very possible that you will begin to feel more comfortable being alone than in companies that do not allow you to grow. Travel and long conversations with friends may give you the light to change partners or rethink the terms of the relationship.

It will be a year of testing, for only those who understand life in a freeway will stay, while those who do not will surely take different paths.

Predictions for Leo

You are not alone; the Guardian Angels want to tell you that they will never leave you. Nothing you thought, said or did, can repel your divine assistants.

Remain calm in your daily life situations, as this year you may continue to experience insomnia. Do not try to embrace more than your strength can resist and you will witness positive changes in your physical and mental health.

Your economy will have momentous changes during this 2024. You should distance yourself from people who, with their attitude, take energy away from you instead of giving it to you. Do not be afraid of novelty, remember that your angel will be willing to help you get a new job in an optimal and accelerated way.

Your angel recommends you concentrate on your work and leave aside the competitiveness of your sign, because all that flow of energy will result in masterpieces if you concentrate.

Your personal brilliance will be unmistakable, sentimental possibilities will multiply, that is why your angels recommend you to be prudent and avoid temptations to focus your energy on the right way.

Virgo Predictions

This year you should choose a profession that you love. The Angels help you to find these talents in you.

Be prepared for unexplainable events and make the most of every opportunity. Wise Angels offer you to get rid of the habit that keeps you from moving forward. Do a variety of things and observe your life with interest. If the path ahead is complicated, function as if you are exploring an unknown place. Angels inspire you, move forward with expectation and hope.

You will have the possibility of creating your sentimental destiny, leaving doubts aside and taking a little more risk.

Keep the necessary precautions since an encouragement or award will make many people envy your triumphs. Your angel recommends reinforcing your self-esteem and recognizing that you are a being full of gifts and deserve the best that the universe can give you.

If you have a stable partner, the end of the year will be a very propitious time to advance in commitments that tend to the union between family groups and reorganization. Large investments supported by your partner will have successful results.

Libra Predictions

It is especially important for you this year 2024. You must meditate more often. To do this, when you wake up in the morning, stay in bed for the first five minutes with your eyes closed and breathe deeply. Talk to them and then listen carefully, what message will be sent to you.

The Angels tell you to stay away from all activities that do not reflect your intentions.

All issues related to your work, relationships, health, will be resolved surprisingly and successfully. Angels will constantly lead you to actions leading to corrections of any negative situation.

Your angel will show you the way to reconciliation with those you have left aside and will remind you that it is a bad idea to separate from those who have shown you constant fidelity.

Some allergies and throat problems may occur.

Your angel will activate your social life to unsuspected limits. Keep a relaxed pace and avoid very demanding exercises.

Scorpio Predictions

This year 2024 you must trust your intuition. This is what the Angels are telling you. The intuitive feelings you feel, the visions, the inner voice, all are attempts to tell you something important, so you must trust and follow these guidelines.

Remember that when you are asked to wait, it means that you have something better than you could ever imagine, prepared just for you. That is why you must change your attitude and accept the situation. Relax.

Ask your Angel to support you throughout this year so that you can listen to divine advice. Do not rush when you see something that may break your will. The next door will open when the time comes, and you will gain new strength.

Angels will help you meet your romantic needs. Ask for their help and accept it. Angels will help you look for the love of your life, they will guide you, telling you the way to fulfill your desires. For example, you may feel an ardent desire to go to a specific place. There you will meet a person with whom you will connect in a love affair.

The Angels also want you to improve your education.

Predictions for Sagittarius

A new chapter begins in your life. You will have a new partner, or an old relationship will be restored. Open your heart to that new feeling of love that will come to you.

Look closely at the people you meet on your path, be open to change in existing relationships and do not get too attached to your old ideas about them. There is a time of wonderful change in your life, so trust the Angels.

Some changes in your life can be painful if you do not show enough flexibility in your thoughts and actions. If you have a new love, remember that the past must remain in the past, away from the new happiness.

Your current relationship may end, or, on the contrary, move into a new phase of renewed love, the Angels ask you to trust them and follow their instructions.

If you already have a close relationship with a person, the Angels are asking you to give them a chance and decide what to do with them, try to develop a next level or end it to make way for a new love. In both cases the Angels will be with you, helping you to choose the right path!

Predictions for Capricorn

It is time to educate yourself. The Angels advise you not to save your strength or time for this activity, but to read, listen and develop yourself.

During this year it is important to dedicate yourself to the acquisition of new knowledge, ideas, and skills. You will want to start learning and if you are currently studying, the Angels are asking you to continue your education.

Sometimes, in the process of acquiring new knowledge and skills, we have a desire to quickly evaluate them in practice, and this leads to the fact that many people drop out of school early, the Angels advise you not to rush things. Continue your education.

The personal growth that accompanies learning can bring you joy if you remember the need in your thoughts to stay here and now.

Ask your angels to help you get rid of the fear of poverty, so you can fully enjoy the growth of abundance. Angels report the influx of abundance in your life. in your life. Continue to believe, this will provide you with constant material, emotional, spiritual, and intellectual support.

Aquarius Predictions

This year relax, grant the Angels a chance to help you. Whatever you give up will be replaced by something better.

You are behaving stubbornly that does not bring you anything good and does not allow happiness and health to enter your life.

If you are unhappy in love, if you are not advancing in your career, have family or financial problems, as well as illness, let the Angels adjust the situation.

If you stubbornly dwell on unfruitful aspects of your life, and fear that things will get worse, they really will. However, if you are willing to free yourself from the situation that oppresses you, the current situation will improve in a wonderful way.

The Angels ask you not to try to control the outcome of your current negative situation. Let it go.

The Angels confirm that, through your own feelings, dreams, visions, and intuition, you really hear them, and these are not hallucinations. If you suddenly have the desire to call someone, go somewhere, read something, it is important that you follow these inner impulses, the Angels ask you to abandon all doubts about divine guidance.

Predictions for Pisces

The Angels know of your past disappointments that have undermined your faith in yourself, others and even the Angels, yet they remind you of the importance of preserving your faith.

The Angels know that you, like everyone else, have made mistakes in the past. These mistakes, however, do not change your true nature. Within you, there is part of the divine nature, which is infallible. The Angels ask you to believe in yourself. Try to make sure that your thoughts and feelings reflect your true intentions.

The Angels ask you to choose your goals carefully and accomplish them with love. Visualize yourself in other happy, successful, and peaceful people. By sticking to highly spiritual intentions, you help yourself and others. The Angels ask you to replace negative thought habits with positive ones, just ask for their help.

About the Authors

In addition to her astrological knowledge, Alina A. Rubi has an abundant professional education; she holds certifications in Psychology, Hypnosis, Reiki, Bioenergetic Crystal Healing, Angelic Healing, Dream Interpretation and is a Spiritual Instructor. Rubi has knowledge of Gemology, which she uses to program stones or minerals and turn them into powerful Amulets or Talismans of protection.

Rubi has a practical and purposeful character, which has allowed her to have a special and integrative vision of several worlds, facilitating solutions to specific problems. Alina writes the Monthly Horoscopes for the website of the American Association of Astrologers; you can read them at www.astrologers.com. At this moment she writes a weekly column in El Nuevo Herald newspaper on spiritual topics, published every Monday in digital and printed form. He also has a program and the weekly Horoscope on the YouTube channel of this newspaper. Her Astrological Yearbook is published every year in the newspaper "Diario las Américas", under the column Rubi Astrologa.

Rubi has authored several articles on astrology for the monthly publication "Today's Astrologer", has taught classes on Astrology, Tarot, Palm Reading, Crystal Healing, and Esotericism. She has weekly videos on esoteric topics on her YouTube channel: Rubi Astrologa. She had her own Astrology show broadcasted daily through Flamingo T.V., has been interviewed by several T.V. and radio programs, and every year she publishes her "Astrological Yearbook" with the horoscope sign by sign, and other interesting mystical topics.

She is the author of the books "Rice and Beans for the Soul" Part I, II, and III, a compilation of esoteric articles, published in English, Spanish, French, Italian and Portuguese. "Money for All Pockets", "Love for All Hearts", "Health for All Bodies, Astrological Yearbook 2021, Horoscope 2022, Rituals and Spells for Success in 2022, and 2023. Spells and Secrets, Astrology Classes, Rituals and Charms 2024 and Chinese Horoscope 2024 are all available in five languages: English, Italian, French, Japanese and German.

Rubi speaks English and Spanish perfectly, combining all her talents and knowledge in her readings. She currently resides in Miami, Florida.

*For more information you can visit **the website** www.esoterismomagia.com*

Alina A. Rubi is the daughter of Alina Rubi. She is currently studying psychology at Florida International University.

Since she was a child, she has been interested in all metaphysical and esoteric subjects and has practiced astrology and Kabbalah since she was four years old. She has knowledge of Tarot, Reiki, and Gemology. She is not only the author, but also the editor, along with her sister Angeline A. Rubi, of all the books published by her and her mother.

*For further information please contact them by email: **rubiediciones29@gmail.com***